D0407773

THE

DAWN

OF

HOPE

THE
DAWN
OF
HOPE

A

MEMOIR

OF

RAVENSBRÜCK

GENEVIÈVE
DE GAULLE ANTHONIOZ

Translated from the French by
RICHARD SEAVER

ARCADE PUBLISHING • NEW YORK

FIRST ENGLISH-LANGUAGE EDITION

First published in France under the title *La Traversée de la
nuit*

Library of Congress Cataloging-in-Publication Data

Gaulle Anthonioz, Geneviève de.
    [Traversée de la nuit.   English]
    The dawn of hope : a memoir of Ravensbrück /
Geneviève de Gaulle Anthonioz ; translated from the
French by Richard Seaver.
  —1st English-language ed.
      p.   cm.
    ISBN 1-55970-498-5
    1. Gaulle Anthonioz, Geneviève de.   2. World War,
1939–1945—Prisoners and prisons, German.   3. World
War, 1939–1945—Personal narratives, French.   4. Ravensbrück (Concentration camp)   I. Title.
940.53'17'092—dc21
[B]   99-38018

Published in the United States by Arcade Publishing, Inc.,
New York
Distributed by Time Warner Trade Publishing

10 9 8 7 6 5 4 3 2 1

Designed by API

BP

PRINTED IN THE UNITED STATES OF AMERICA

"Everything begins again, everything is true."

Publisher's Note

Geneviève de Gaulle, who was born in 1920, is the niece of General Charles de Gaulle, who led the Free French Forces during World War II and later became president of France. When the Germans invaded and overran France in 1940, Geneviève, then nineteen, immediately joined the Resistance movement. Three years later, on July 20, 1943, she was arrested in Paris and incarcerated in Fresnes Prison, one of the country's worst. Six months later, on February 3, 1944, she was shipped in one of the legendary cattle cars to Ravensbrück concentration camp, where she was matriculated under the number 27.372. She remained in Ravens-brück, a good deal of the time in solitary confinement, until the end of the war.

For fifty years Geneviève resisted the efforts of her family and friends to have her record her wartime memoirs. But last year, at the age of seventy-eight, her memories overwhelmed her, or at least overcame her reticence, and in the space of less than three weeks, they, as it were, dictated themselves to her. The result is a brief but startlingly powerful book, which critics have hailed as a "work of incredible force," a "punch in the solar plexus," a "flash of lightning in the night sky," a "stunning incarnation of the spirit of resistance," and (by Jorge Semprun, former Spanish minister of culture and author of the prize-winning concentration-camp memoir *The Long Voyage*), "unforgettable."

Not a Jew but a Christian, Geneviève de Gaulle brings to the long line of Holocaust literature a searing new document demonstrating how, in the face of total, unimaginable Evil, the human spirit can survive.

In 1975, commemorating the thirtieth anniversary of the liberation of the German camps, André Malraux, then French minister of culture, said in a speech to camp survivors:

> And in those death camps you discovered that the will to live was, however obscurely, anchored deep within yourselves. Without the least defense, stripped of your humanity, the only way you could bear witness was by staying alive. And that you somehow managed to do.

After the war, Geneviève married Bernard Anthonioz and had three children. But the images and memories of Ravensbrück refused to leave her, and in 1958 she met Father Joseph Wrensinski, a priest who years earlier had been homeless and had dedicated his life to helping the destitute—not just those who were poor but those beyond poverty: the homeless, the socially excluded. The first time Geneviève accompanied Father Wrensinski to the outskirts of Paris—to a shantytown where the homeless were living in makeshift tin-and-cardboard shacks—she suddenly saw in their eyes the same dull glaze, the same expression of utter despair that she had seen in the eyes of her fellow prisoners in Ravensbrück. These destitute humans, like her fellow inmates, had left all hope behind. From that day on she dedicated her life to bringing hope back into their lives, light back into their eyes. She became involved in, and later president of, an organization known as ATD, Aid in Total Distress, which later evolved into a larger entity known as ATD Fourth World. Today that organization, begun in a French shantytown just outside the world's most glittering metropolis, operates in eight European countries, North and South America, and several countries in Asia and Africa.

THE

DAWN

OF

HOPE

*T*he door closes heavily behind me. I am alone in the night. I can scarcely make out the bare walls of my cell. Groping blindly in the dark, I make my way to the wooden platform and its rough-textured blanket and lie back down, trying to summon up again my interrupted dream: a while ago I was walking along a moonlit road—a light so soft, so healing—and voices were calling to me. Then suddenly there was nothing but the beam of a flashlight, the frightened face of our barracks chief, the harsh order for me to get to my feet, and the shadows of two SS men. Nightmare or reality? Baty and Felicity, whose straw mattresses lay next to mine on either side, woke up as well. They gathered up my few belongings, including my tin cup and bowl, helped me down from the bunk, and hugged me in their arms. What is this all about? What does it mean for me? I know that executions take place in the dead of night.

For the time being, I am in a building inside the Ravensbrück concentration camp called the bunker. It's a prison within the prison, which also serves as a solitary confinement cell. Here there is no blanket, no straw mattress; bread is handed out every three days, soup once every five days. When you are sent to solitary, your welcome is often a flogging: twenty-five strokes, fifty strokes, seventy-five strokes, from which the prisoner rarely survives. In the camp proper, we are fully aware of that, as we are aware of the fact that in this place—in the bunker—Professor Gebhardt is conducting his horrible experiments, using young women as human guinea pigs.

Since despite all my efforts I cannot fall asleep again, I start thinking about our seventy-five little "rabbits" (*Kaninchen* is what we call them here). Their legs are horribly mutilated, they hop and jump about with the help of makeshift crutches. These young Polish girls (the youngest, Bacha, is fourteen) have been operated on, some as many as half a dozen times. The renowned surgeon, a Berlin University professor, has operated on both their bones and their muscles, then infected their wounds with gangrene, tetanus, and streptococcus. Through his experiments he attempted to prove that Gauleiter Heydrich, whom he treated after an attempt on his life, could not have survived the infections to his wounds.

After the initial series of "operations," the prisoners had put up some kind of resistance to avoid going under the knife again. But they were quickly trussed up and bundled off to the bunker, where Dr. Gebhardt continued his surgical experiments without anesthesia and without any aseptic treatment. Now that I'm here, where it all took place, I have a better idea of what they must have gone through, how unimaginable their suffering must have been.

When I hear the first wail of the siren, I know it is half past three in the morning. In the overcrowded barracks, the daytime nightmare is again beginning. The scuffle for the distribution of "coffee," the jostling to gain access to the disgusting latrines, which are pitifully few in number, before the second siren sounds for roll call. It is October 29, and the weather is holding up reasonably well, not yet terribly cold. But how endless it seems, standing there for the camp roll calls to be over! If the numbers don't tally because during the night someone has died and they have forgotten to erase her name from the ledger (when this happens, the body has to be carried immediately out to the camp square), we sometimes stand there for hours without moving. And suddenly that makes me think that my sudden nocturnal departure for solitary confinement may not yet have been brought to the attention of the authorities. I am sure that Baty and Felicity will not yet have had time to let my friends know. They have no idea what has become of me, and here I have to confront that fate, whatever it may be, without their tenderness and compassion. And with that thought, a feeling of total solitude runs through me like an icy blade.

A few days ago we celebrated my birthday together. To make the cake, everyone contributed a handful of bread crumbs, which we kneaded together with several spoonfuls of the molasseslike substance they call "jam" or "jelly." For candles, we used twenty-four twigs, and for decoration some leaves we had furtively and hastily picked along the banks of the swamp during our work convoys there. A true moment of happiness!

Another siren, meaning roll call is over and the work columns are setting off for the day. From the depths of my night I can hear the dull thud of the wooden soles, the distant barking of dogs, and the harsh shouts of the SS guards. Here I am, far away, as if at the bottom of a deep well where, little by little, I will fade away and die. And if the door were to open, would it be for me to walk toward the corridor where the executions take place? It's not far away, just on the other side of the crematorium ovens, whose stacks send forth their wreaths of smoke into the sky.

Must I prepare myself for death? No one will be there to help or comfort me, to hold my hand as I so often have held others' during the final moments of one of my fellow prisoners. The last faces I shall see will be filled with hate and contempt. Don't think about it any more and, obviously, put your family out of your mind or you'll lose courage. More difficult to take leave of Germaine, of Jacqueline, of Danielle, of Milena, of Greta, of so many others whose fraternal affection has enabled me to survive till now. Will they ever know how I died? A dress riddled with bullet holes, stained with blood, one more name crossed off the camp list: that is how we learned of the fate of the others who disappeared into the night.

But what about those who are still here? What will become of them? Will *any* of them survive? What terrible trials and tribulations will we have to face over the coming months? We know the invasion has occurred, that the Allies have landed in France; even the SS newspaper had to admit that. But since then all we know is that fierce combats are still taking place. The thought of spending another winter here is simply unbearable.

I make an effort to pray: "Our Father, Who art in heaven . . ." "Hail, Mary, full of grace . . ." fragments of the psalms. From the depths of the abyss, I too call out to God, as so many others have before me. I try to deliver myself over to the boundless mercy of the Father, to make myself one with the agony of Jesus in the Garden of Olives. In response, it is not even a silence I hear, but the wretched and distant murmur of my own distress.

I'm ashamed to confess, but I *am* afraid, afraid of those moments that will mark the end of my life. But isn't that the only way not to be alone any longer—by sharing the anguish of those who, like me, are destined to die today? Massacred by the blows of a pickax, bitten by dogs, thrown into ditches like dirt or refuse. I have seen it with my own eyes, heard the frightful moans and laments without being able to lift a finger to help. Now I belong to those who have lost all hope. Together we cry out, like Christ on the cross, "Oh, God, why hast thou forsaken me?"

From the corridor just outside my cell

door, I can hear the sound of boots on concrete and the click of keys opening cell-door grates. Doubtless food is being handed out to those who have the right to receive it. But for me, nothing! Obviously, if they are planning to kill me in the near future, what's the point of feeding me? My eyes have to some degree adjusted to the darkness. I have made a search of my cell, felt my way along the clammy walls, made a mental inventory of what it contains: a shelf, a stool chained to the wall, a toilet of sorts, above which is a spigot. I manage to find my tin cup and take a long drink of water, which gives me great pleasure, even if it turns out that it will be my last drink on earth.

Figuring there's no point trying to remain alert, on my guard, I finally manage to fall asleep and don't wake up until I hear the evening siren. My comrades are coming back, dead with fatigue from the day's labors. They are made to march in rows, five abreast, in martial cadence with, if they are the building contingent, their shovels slung over their shoulders. When my convoy arrived in February, the guards ordered us to sing, so we did; but when we broke into a French military marching song they were less than appreciative! For several months I worked in the swamp, once and a while in the forest. The worst job was loading railroad cars with coal in July, when it was unbearably hot, with never any possibility of washing up. The pace of the work was extremely tough, but there was always the threat of the guards' truncheons, not to mention the dogs, and the twelve-hour work shift went on without a break.

We did manage to find a bit of solace in nature: some sprigs of herbs and plants culled for the vitamins they contained, sometimes even a flower clandestinely brought back to the camp for someone who was bedridden or to celebrate a birthday. On our way to and from our work stations, we walked through the SS village; the children belted us with stones as we passed. After that, we walked around the lake; the countryside was sad and beautiful: sand, birch trees, and pines.

When I was taken off the earthwork convoy and sent to work inside, at first I breathed a sigh of relief, thinking I had found a less demanding job. In the barracks workshop, our job was to take the uniforms that had been sent back from the Eastern front—taken from the bodies of the wounded and dead—and salvage from them whatever we could. The fact that the uniforms were in tatters, that they contained vestiges of human remains and were filled with lice, did not mean we could not glean something useful from them—buttons, the lining—all of which could be recycled. When we came into the barracks for the first time, we were greeted with an enormous pile of this clothing. Under the watchful eyes of the SS guards, we had to cut and snip, unstitch anything deemed salvageable while the SS urged us on: *"Schnell, schnell, schnell!"* Other prisoners had the job of washing whatever we had managed to salvage. The stench was unbearable, and the SS man in charge of us was one of the worst in the camp. Once I saw a poor woman in our work group who surreptitiously dared to wash a piece of her own linen. The SS happened to see what she was up to; he took out his truncheon and beat her to death on the spot. The beating seemed to go on forever before she finally succumbed.

It didn't take me long to wish I was back with the outdoor work group, all the more so because I was assigned to the clothing-salvage barracks one week on the day shift and the following week on the night shift. And then everything began to go downhill for me: I contracted both scurvy and corneal ulcerations; I was suffering so much physically that I could never manage to keep up with my work quota. The

SS guard, whose name was Syllinka, knew how to deal with me: in the course of my week on the night shift, he beat me savagely several times. Before long I would surely be killed like the woman who had tried to wash her undies. Meanwhile, my wounds were suppurating, so much so that they spilled onto the uniforms that had been shipped in from the fields of battle, some of which I had managed to slip under me on my chair to ease my pain.

But for the time being I have managed to escape any further blows from Syllinka's ready hand. The question is: at what cost? To die here in solitary confinement, or nearby in the execution corridor? Or perhaps I'm simply fated to die of hunger. From what I understand, if you are deprived of food and only drink a bit of water, you slip, little by little, into an endless sleep. Here I have as much water as I want from my spigot, a thin stream that has a strange taste but one that has obsessed me so often during the torrid heat of summer days.

Tonight will mark my third night in this cell. At last, I'm beginning to grow accustomed to it. My eyes no longer suffer from the bright sunlight. No more pushing and shoving to get to the latrines or into the coffee line, no more truncheon blows, no more constant harassment day and night. I have a bunk to myself; I can sleep. Dreamless nights, profound as black water, pierced by the siren's wail. Do you know, my comrades, that I am with you, close beside you? I feel your bone-weariness, I see through your eyes the pearly dawn that lightens the sky above the horizon of the Baltic. There is no other life to dream of than yours, than ours. Beyond lies the unattainable. Limit your dream to still being alive, to sharing the tainted drinking water, the hard, gray bread, the soup in which, if you are lucky, a turnip or two might be swimming . . . and, above all, limit your dream to the comfort of a handshake, the tenderness of a loving look. When the dread hour comes to awaken to a new day, listen to Jacqueline as she breaks into song: "Awake O sleeping hearts, the Lord is calling you. . . . " The memory of her clear soprano voice makes me sing in turn and tempts me to pray, here in my desert, here in my night.

When I was in Fresnes Prison on the outskirts of Paris, and even later during the endless voyage to Ravensbrück, once in a while there was a response to my prayers, a ray of hope. But as we entered the camp, it was as though God had remained outside. By the light of the projectors, we caught a glimpse of women carrying heavy vats. I could barely make out their unsteady silhouettes, their shaven heads, but I was thunderstruck by the vision of their faces, which has remained with me ever since. Never had I seen—on the faces of those sentenced to death, those who had been or were about to be tortured—anyone so indelibly marked by inhuman distress. These human beings, though still alive, had already lost every vestige of expression. I should have felt compassion for them, but what overwhelmed me was a feeling of utter despair. "You who enter here, leave all hope behind," wrote Dante in the *Inferno*.

As we walked, or rather staggered, bone-weary between the dark camp barracks day in and day out, across the black cinders of the ground beneath our feet, I was struck with the absolute certainty that there was indeed a fate far worse than death: the destruction of our souls, which was the purpose and goal of the concentration-camp universe.

From that point on, what did the knowledge that death was imminent matter? For nine months I struggled not to yield to despair, to maintain my own self-respect and that of my fellow prisoners. No, God was not absent, He shed His light on Emilie Tillions's lovely face; old Maria, Sister Elizabeth, were radiant in His reflected light. Clandestinely, we stole behind one of the barracks with a Roman Orthodox nun—a former and fanatic revolutionary—to pray together; Sister Mary and she had responded to the ordeal of the camp by moving to a higher level of spiritual communion.

Here in my cell I do my humble best to follow in their wake. But in no way do I want to try to detach myself in my prayers from the most wretched among them— those who stole bread, who elbowed their fellow inmates aside to make sure they got their allotted ration of soup, or, worse yet, those who lay helpless in some corner with their vermin and filth. They are the reflection of what we came so close to becoming, and we must share their humiliation as I do our fraternity and bread.

I slip into a state of total lethargy, from which I'm awakened by the sound of my cell door being unlocked. Standing in the doorway is a female guard who looks at me in amazement.

"Who are you? What are you doing here? How long have you been here?"

My knowledge of German enables me to understand her questions and formulate a response. The woman leaves and goes off to try to find out what I'm doing here, then comes back shortly to inform me that I'm the victim of an error. I've been "overlooked" since my arrival in solitary. I'm not being punished and my failure to be given food will be rectified shortly. She also tells me that the shutters covering my window, which keeps me in almost total darkness, will be reopened.

An elderly female inmate soon arrives with some food. She is wearing the purple triangle that marks her a member of Jehovah's Witnesses, and her camp number indicates that she has been here a long time, probably one of the earliest inmates. With the shutter open, a faint light trickles in, enabling me for the first time to see my new living quarters. Though cold and damp, the cell is clean, and I see that for cellmates I have a bevy of fat cock-roaches, that seem totally uninterested in me until my meager ration of bread ar-rives.

Since apparently I'm going to go on liv-ing, I have to get myself organized: not wolf down my food, chew slowly no matter how hungry I am. Also try to exercise a lit-tle. There's a chair that enables me to crack open the transom; behind the thick glass, which is opaque, is a grill, then a set of bars. I figure out that I'm in the under-ground portion of the solitary section; these barred windows must open onto a ditch that separates the prison from the barracks of the SS guards. Impossible for anyone from the camp to make contact with me. And who, I wonder, are my fel-low inmates here in solitary? No one re-sponds when I knock on my left-hand wall or cry out with my face pressed close to the stones; on the other side are probably some poor wretches from the camp being punished. I finally figure out that the cell immediately to my right is occupied by an SS soldier, which ended any attempt at communication on that side! As we learned in the camp, the solitary section was also used as a maximum security prison for men. Who could escape from it, set as it was in the center of a women's concentration camp?

It doesn't take me long to make a list of my few possessions: a fairly large piece of white cloth stolen by my friend Bérengère as she was unloading the bags of clothing of those who had been exterminated at Auschwitz. To her I also owe the sweater I'm wearing beneath my striped prison dress. My only pair of thick wool stockings was knitted by Lisa, who, at her risk and peril, liberated the yarn from one of the workshops. Miraculously, my needle holder, which was given me for my birthday by Violaine and which I had hidden in my sleeve as I left the barracks, is still intact, containing three steel needles: one with white thread, another with black, and the third with red. All of this precious material was carefully kept concealed from Syllinka's watchful eye, as was the piece of leather I have that came from the visor of a tank officer's cap. I also have a little cloth pouch for my ration of bread, and in the hem of my skirt is sequestered a tiny pencil. My other little presents have wisely been left behind in the care of my barracksmate Baty: in all likelihood, I'll never see them again.

Another interesting discovery: what serves as toilet paper (what luxury!) are little squares cut out from the newspaper. I read some news items that are fairly dated and put several aside so that I can later fill in the blanks where the news has been censored.

I duly note that today is All Saints Day. Last year at this time, at Fresnes, the German military chaplain had celebrated Mass for those prisoners not in solitary. When one of us read aloud the Beatitudes, there was so much peace and joy in the room I felt I was among the blessed of the earth. I search my memory for the divine words to no avail . . . their light has been extinguished, my heart as hard as a rock inside me. In vain do I invoke the names of the saints. They have become as foreign to me as mathematical formulas.

On November 2, I force myself to dwell on our family dead: my dear, darling mother, whom I was made to kiss, all cold in her coffin, in the midst of Father's tears and those of his entire family. She was so tender, so gentle, so happy—no, it was not Mother lying there beneath the taut, white sheet. I fled into the garden, where the irises had been cut, in order to bedeck her coffin. In one fell swoop, a little four-year-old girl learned the meaning of unhappiness. My sister was three, my brother, two. On each of our hats my grandmother had sewn a little white daisy with a golden heart. Mama died in the Sarre Department, where Papa worked as an engineer. We made a long voyage to Anjou, where she was to be buried. The funeral wagon, marked in chalk with a white cross, was hooked up to our train. Papa took us by the hand to her car so we could see her. Why did he say, "That's where your mother is"?—in this pitch-black train car, completely closed, as later were the cattle cars of the deportation convoy.

In 1938, just after the Munich Accords, it was my sister's turn to leave us. She was only seventeen, blond with blue eyes, a girl who loved life to the hilt. We shared a bedroom, and then, suddenly, her bed was empty. They came and removed from our closet her clothes, which were almost identical to mine.

At the Fresnes Prison, from the scraps of newspaper hidden in the hem of my underwear, I learned of the death of my grandmother. She was buried in the same grave as my mother and sister, where

Grandmother's children, who had died before her, were also buried.

Many of my comrades have a hard time accepting the idea that their ashes will end up in the neighboring peat marshes. As for myself, I found the morgue, where the bodies are piled one on top of the other, far more repelling. Besides, death isn't the worst thing here: the worst is the hate and the violence. I tried with all my might to avoid looking at the nightmare faces. We were strictly forbidden from looking directly at the SS guards, but when one of them gave full vent to his fury, mercilessly attacking some poor wretch a mere few feet from us, it was impossible to avoid seeing the terrible look of pleasure in their faces.

All night long I am obsessed by the same vision: heads floating in a sea of blood, and on each of their faces an unspeakably ugly smile. I awake with a vision of a big magnolia tree covered with flowers. It was under such a tree that a woman friend told me that my mother was dead. Then, strangely, my cell is filled with the smell of magnolia blossoms!

The days go by amazingly quickly, whereas each moment seems interminable. In the morning, during roll call, the guard cracks open my door; I am obliged to stand at attention, without moving a muscle, as called for by the camp rules. After that, I don't see anyone, only a rare glimpse of the old lady who passes me my soup through the grill. The soup is the same as the one they gave us in camp—just as bad but slightly thicker. One day I chance upon a tiny piece of meat floating in the soup and I burst into tears, thoroughly astonished at myself for such utter lack of self-control.

One day the guard takes me for a very short walk in a tiny internal courtyard, where I get my first glimpse of the sky in a long time. It is a leaden, gray sky, which feels like snow. In fact, the first flakes begin to fall; then I hear the order for me to return to my cell, to the oppressive walls of my prison, to its darkness, its silence. When I get back inside, again I burst into tears.

My eyes close into a kind of interior vision: a big, peaceful lake in the middle of a dark forest. The shores of the lake are steep and bare. Not a reed, not a ripple, not a bird. Fascinated, I move dangerously forward. A strong hand holds me back and prevents me from falling. And suddenly a feeling of enormous peace washes over me. I only wish I could share the feeling! The chant of Hail Mary comes back to me, every last word of it; Mother of mercy, our salvation, our hope, has turned her eyes toward this poor creature who is moaning and weeping. I ask her to be merciful to those who suffer or are in despair, those for whom the specter of death looms nigh, those near and dear to me, about whom I have no news whatsoever. It's the first time since October 28 that I have felt so close to them.

I note each passing day in the margin of a newspaper page. Advent is fast approaching, which means Christmas is only a month away. To try to trick my sense of boredom, I decide to organize some cockroach races. From the whole troop, two champions emerge. Now I can tell them apart: the biggest cockroach is Victor, the other one I name Felix. For the also-rans I save a few crumbs as consolation prizes. There is a brief moment before night falls when a pale light filters through my "skylight," at least on clear days. My fellow inmates in solitary here must see the same light, if they are still alive.

One Sunday afternoon, the elderly inmate who brings me my meals opens the door of my cell and switches on a light. In a low voice she tells me that the SS are having some sort of celebration—that they're very much in their cups—and says she'd like to take the opportunity to give me what I need to repair my poor stockings. I gratefully accept her offer, and she hands me a bit of wool yarn, a needle, and scissors. The stockings are full of holes, some of which are major, and I thank the good sisters who, when I was at boarding school, taught me how to mend and darn stockings. When the Jehovah's Witness lady returns to collect her material, she utters a little cry of admiration. . . . If I like, she'll bring some more sewing supplies; which she does: on several occasions she slips me yarn and scissors and needles, which I use to mend all my clothes. The lady's name is Anna, I learn ("Please call me Anna"), and I make up my mind to embroider a little napkin for her as a Christmas present, for Christmas is just around the corner. In preparation for this, I draw with my pencil stub a kind of picture. It's my manger: the Christ child is leaning against a cross, one finger raised in a sign of benediction. A woman deportee in her striped camp dress and head scarf is leaning up against Him. Under a triangle marked with an "F" I write out the number 27.372: my concentration camp ID number.

In vain I try to chase from my mind all memory of Christmases past, especially the one that followed the death of my mother, when Father sang the Christmas carols that mother had written out in her own hand. We looked down at our little shoes, happy despite all that had happened, and thanked the Christ Child and Mother for all the presents that heaven had sent us. Father fled from the room in tears. For Christmas last year, at Fresnes Prison, the chaplain celebrated Mass as he had done on All Saints Day, and the chapel was adorned with pine branches. For my convoy, which reached Ravensbrück on February 3, this will be our first Christmas in the camp. Each of us will do our best not to sink into depression, make an effort to cheer one another up—even mothers whose children have been taken away from them. Hadn't we all promised ourselves and each other a thousand times that no matter what, "We'll surely be home by Christmas"?

Will the SS newspaper possibly let a bit of good news filter through? When I was sent down here to solitary, there were some inmates who claimed we were going to be liberated very soon. . . . What was "soon"? In a month, in a week, the following day? . . . In fact, they were right about the dates but wrong about the information: what those dates really signified was how long most of them had left to live. And the children? What about the gypsy girls whose mothers had consented to their sterilization so that they would be allowed to live—will they celebrate Christmas in some fashion? And what will this holiday mean for the babies who by some stroke of luck have not been taken from their mothers at birth to be forcibly drowned? They have survived, but day by day Marie-Jo watches them slowly waste away because their mothers have no milk to feed them. On December 25, as on every other day, mothers will trudge to the morgue bearing the bodies of the babies for whom this is not a day of birth but of death.

I have finished the handkerchief for Anna, and in one corner I embroider her camp number. Tomorrow morning I'll slip it into her hand as she passes my coffee through the grill; then I shall at least have given a present, exchanged a smile with a fellow human being.

The twenty-fourth of December is sadder and longer than any other day. It starts off with the clang of doors being opened and shut, then I hear cries and moans, after which, silence, which strikes me as even more terrifying than all the noises that went before. Then all of a sudden a woman's voice is heard singing:

Silent Night, Holy Night,
All is calm, all is bright.

Where is the voice coming from? Is it a prisoner? A female guard? No matter. Blessed be that voice, for that song has brought with it a moment of peace. Before I fall asleep, I too sing several carols: "O Holy Night," "It Came upon a Midnight Clear," "O Come All Ye Faithful," "Angels We Have Heard on High".... But I refuse to sing "O Christmas Tree," for the pine trees of Meklemburg offer us no peace.

I was dreaming that Violaine was with me when the siren for roll call woke me up. No. I'm alone, and I remember the present I made for Anna. This morning there is no roll call for work camp, and I can hear them talking and serving coffee earlier than usual. I station myself by the door, and as soon as Anna opens the grill I slip the handkerchief into her hand and in German wish her Merry Christmas. No smile, no response; all I can do is sadly drink my coffee. Once again, my eyes are filled with tears. There is no question of my feeling sorry for myself. Today we are celebrating the Word of God, He who came unto us in the form of a child and descended to live among us. Yes, even in this place of desolation, where fear and wickedness reign supreme. If from the depths of my despair I cry out to Him, perhaps will He make His voice known to me, perhaps will I be touched by the sweetness of His love. But no, there is no reply, or if there is I fail to hear it.

Unto us a child is born,
A Son is given unto us.

He was born to succor the most wretched among us as He was born for the cruelest of the SS guards: for Syllinka, for Ruth Neudeck, whom I have seen slit the throat of an inmate with the sharp edge of her shovel. There are no Christmas carols, even those of the angels themselves, capable of drowning out the laments, the screams, the cries of anger and hate. Nor is there any way for me to get away, to transcend myself; my manger is here in this solitary cell that separates me from the camp but that, little by little, is filled with frightful images and terrible rumors.

The following day the cell door opens, and, to my amazement, who do I see come in but Anna. Her face is wreathed in a broad smile, and she walks over and puts a small box on my straw mattress.

"From your friends," she says. "A Christmas present from your friends. I couldn't bring it to you any sooner, because we were being watched by the SS guards even more closely than usual. But now they are sleeping off their long night of heavy drinking and debauchery. I managed to get hold of the key. Take everything out of the box. I'll stop by a little later to pick it up."

Wonder of wonders! There is a little

branch of a pine tree, a French Christmas carol, four cookies cut in the form of a star, a shiny red apple, a tiny piece of pork fat, two squares of sugar. And then there is a doll, a marquise, all dressed up in a pink shirt and lace scarf, with curly white hair. Beneath her skirt is embroidered a "J" and an "A". Jacqueline d'Alincourt, of course, my sister prisoner, who is sending me this present. And as for the French Christmas carol—"Away in a Manger"— that is from Anicka, with the help of Vlasta. Their friendship is so strong they were able to accomplish the miracle of reaching out to me in my solitude and despair. And last but not least, at the very bottom of the box, is a neatly folded light-brown shawl made of soft wool, which I immediately wrap around myself as if I were folding myself in their warm and gentle friendship.

Anna returns to pick up the empty box.

"It wasn't a very Merry Christmas! Last night was so sad, the air filled as it was with all the screamings and moanings because of the floggings. Here in the solitary section you were spared, but your neighbors in the camp were not. For Christmas Eve, beatings were the order of the day."

When the cell door closes behind her I am no longer all alone. My comrades have reminded me of this chain of fraternity that links us all together in a common bond. Night falls, and I wrap myself up in the Christmas shawl. It's the first time in two months that I haven't been cold, and in my dream I'm walking through a huge field of white daisies in full bloom, then in a wood of scattered pine trees whose slender trunks shine brightly. It's summertime, and I'm nine or ten years old. My uncle, who is only eleven years older than I and who is also my godfather, weaves me a crown of leaves.

"You're the queen of the flowers, Geneviève. . . . " Filled with happiness, I laugh wholeheartedly; my brother and sister look at me with admiration. When I wake up, I remember that my sister is dead, and I have no idea whether my brother is still alive or not. All I know is that he managed to make it across the Spanish border and volunteered for the Free French Forces. Together, on June 17, 1940, he and I had listened with a mixture of indignation and complete amazement to Marshal Pétain's radio address to the nation. How in the world could one accept this cowardly defeat suffered virtually without putting up any resistance?

Roger was seventeen; I was nineteen. The following day we were part of the mass exodus from Paris, on the roads of Brittany with so many other refugees. We had seen the first German soldiers: a motorcycle contingent with their black jackets and black helmets. How humiliating. My father was beside himself with anger, as were several reserve officers, some of whom were well along in years and none of whom was equipped with any weapon whatsoever. My grandmother was with us, she who as a little girl had wept bitter tears over the French defeat in 1870 at Sedan at the hands of the Prussians. From the far end of a little square in a village through which we passed, a priest came running to tell us an important piece of news: he had just heard over Radio London about a young French general who had made it to that city and was calling on the French to keep on fighting.

"His name," the priest said, "is General de Gaulle."

Grandmother, who was very frail, drew herself up to her full height—which still didn't make her very tall—and tugged the sleeve of the priest. "Father," she said, "that's my son you're talking about. That's my son, Father!"

One month later she was dead, but not before she had heard General de Gaulle's voice several times coming to us via the BBC. She was so proud of him and believed his every word with all her heart and soul.

In the depths of my dark dungeon, I can see again her flower-bedecked grave: day in and day out people we don't even know lay flowers on her tomb.

Never for a moment did she harbor the slightest doubt that her family would follow the path of honor, which meant joining the Resistance. During her final hours, she had said to me, "I suffer for my son." She had three other sons and a daughter, and she had no idea what had become of any of them. But Charles, whose mission it was to take up the sword and hold it high, was always in the forefront of her thoughts. Now, in the Ravensbrück bunker, my role is the offering of my life, another way of rejoining the battle.

For me, the new year—1945—began marked by the echoes of another round of hard drinking on the part of our SS guards. How was the war progressing? In the camp, no matter how hard they tried to keep news from us, we somehow always managed to get wind of what was happening. For instance, I knew about the liberation of Paris the same evening of the day Allied troops marched down the Champs-Elysées. How did I learn so quickly? A Czech friend of mine, Vlasty, who worked in one of the SS offices, had taken advantage of a momentary lapse in the officers' close surveillance to slip over to the office radio—which was always kept on at a very low volume as a precaution, in order to keep the SS constantly informed about possible air raids—and turn up the volume. For a brief second she heard the immense uproar of the people of Paris celebrating their liberation. After work she managed to find me and pass on the news, after which I went to several barracks where the French women were housed and told them that Paris had been liberated.

In remembering these glorious moments, I am far away from my cell. But some disturbing noises in the corridor bring me back to harsh reality. Several days before, my heavy cell door was literally torn asunder from top to bottom by a sudden burst of gunfire. I glued my eye to the crack in the door and saw several men in white blouses scurrying to and fro. I scarcely had time to leave my observation post when the bolts of my cell door were drawn back and I had the unexpected visit of one of those men in white, who entered my cell with a syringe in his hand. He motioned for me to open my dress and gave me an injection directly into the chest. What could it be? A lethal injection such as they administer to those in the camp they judge to be insane or who are suffering from tuberculosis? Or was it an injection in preparation for some medical experiment they intended to perform on me, the way they have on their little rabbits? I had no choice but to wait, and the wait seemed endless. Must I get ready to die? Suddenly, death seemed to me imminent. What pained me most was that no one would know how I met my end—not my father, my family, my friends. I remained standing as long as I could, thinking that I might as well be standing in front of a firing squad. Finally, when I could stand up no longer, I collapsed onto my straw mattress and immediately fell asleep, waking up only when I heard the wail of the siren. It was not the wake-up call but the siren announcing an air raid. The sound of bombs bursting not very far off. Was it possible the war was getting closer? Come now, I thought, you have to try and stay alive: it takes very little to rekindle a taste for living.

When I was in the camp, books were, of course, strictly forbidden but nonetheless available, thanks to the daring of some of our fellow inmates who clandestinely went through the luggage of the arriving prisoners and managed, despite the tight security, to bring an occasional book or two back to the barracks. For several hours I had in my possession a German edition of *Moby Dick;* on another occasion I had an anthology of French poetry, and later a copy of Flaubert's *Salambô*. And there I was, suddenly transported to Africa, basking in the African sun at the foot of the walls of Carthage. Hamilcar's war seemed to me as actual as the one being fought that day. Time ceased to exist, the border between dream and reality, nightmare and reality, disappeared. I could walk out of my cell, cover vast distances of space, travel through centuries of time. Sometimes my mind brought flooding back terrible memories, those I lived scarcely a few weeks before, and then again I was completely consumed by imaginary concerns, such as those brought on by the huge octopus in *Twenty Thousand*

Leagues under the Sea. I fought by trying to recite full stanzas of poems, but more often than not I couldn't remember all the words, and I would end up with fragments of several poems all jumbled together:

The heron rubs shoulders with the strand. . . .
Beneath the Mirabeau Bridge flows the Seine,
  and our love. . . .
Or is it the Gallic Loire,
    the Latin Tiber from afar?
The vast ocean stretches out before me. . . .
O sea, O endless sea . . .

I am carried away by the flood of words: the beam of a lighthouse sweeps across the crest of the waves; the sky is strewn with stars—some I can recognize, but I can't find Altair, in the constellation Aquila. . . . I am stretched out on my back and can feel the warm summer earth beneath me. Suddenly a thick fog moves in and covers everything until it lifts, revealing a huge snow-covered forest. My grandmother and I are in a big sled, drawn by two large horses. The sleigh bells are jingling cheerfully, unless it's the sound of the crystal trees. We're huddled close together under a red shag blanket.

Despite these escapes into fantasy, the days are interminable. I keep a sharp lookout for the little evening light that shines through my air hole, but in vain; nothing comes to lighten my darkness. But that same darkness must be good for my eyes, for the violent pain caused by my corneal ulcerations has almost vanished. On the other hand, I have more and more trouble swallowing any food, and as a result I increase my cockroaches' bread rations. Speaking of which, they are becoming more and more friendly: at one point I discover Felix lodged in the hollow of my arm. Impossible to finish my soup, and I end up throwing it down into the stinking toilet hole. If only I could share it with those women whom I have seen down on their knees, licking up the remains of a turnip soup that spilled onto the floor when a mob of famished women who had been fighting to fill their bowls overturned one of the pots. Compared to what my comrades have to go through every day, I feel privileged. I'm not being beaten, I don't have to work till I drop, I don't have to push and shove for everything I need. I have a straw mattress that is mine and mine alone, as much water as I want, and I can drink to my heart's content and wash up whenever I feel like it.

One morning when it's time for roll call, I don't get to my feet as the rules require each inmate must: stand at attention in front of her bunk. All night long I've been shaking with cold and fever, and there's no way I can drag myself to my feet. The guard who checks me through the peephole sees that I'm still lying there on my mattress and opens the cell door. I cringe for the blows that I know will follow, but instead she simply asks me if I'm not feeling well. A few hours later, much to my surprise, I receive a visit from one of the SS doctors whom I've never seen before. Without setting foot in the cell, he begins to question me. I describe, as briefly as possible, how I'm feeling— fever, an excruciating pain in my right lung—and I venture a guess that I'm probably suffering from another bout of pleurisy, which I had suffered when I first arrived at Ravensbrück. I can't get over the fact that anyone cares! As a result of his visit, for the next two days I'm given four pills and allowed to remain lying down on my mattress.

Roughly three months earlier, on October 3 of the preceding year, my fate had already taken a surprising turn. That day, as I returned exhausted from my work detail, a woman guard had appeared at the door to our wretched and overcrowded barracks and called out my name. After having verified my camp registration number, she ordered me to follow her, but not with the usual brutishness of such commands. The camp commander wanted to see me, she said. We walked through the main gate of the camp, beyond which lay the buildings housing the SS offices, the nearest of which was that of the Kommandant himself. The only times I had ever seen the camp commander, whose name was Suhren, were from afar. He was a formidable personage greatly to be feared. In his presence I had to lower my head and identify myself in German, not with my name—for I was no longer a person—but my inmate number: 27.372. He was standing in front of his desk, in a long room lighted by three windows. His surprising first question was:

"How are you feeling?"

What in the world could have prompted this all-powerful camp master to inquire about the health of such a miserable person as myself, who could be of no possible interest to him? I responded:

"Very poorly, thank you. As you can see."

This unreal dialogue went on.

"Yes, I can see. And you don't look at all well. What is your work detail?"

I told him I worked in the Syllinka Kommando, which was still my official posting. In fact, I had been saved by Milena Seborova, a Czech forewoman, with the help and complicity of Herr Schmidt. The latter had in civilian life been the proprietor of a major ready-to-wear clothing factory in Berlin. Mobilized shortly before the war, Schmidt found himself posted in the SS without anyone ever asking him whether he wanted to be or not. Milena had insinuated herself into his good graces and now had a great deal of influence with him. She kept him posted on the Allied victory and kept dangling before him what his fate would be once the war was over. Half out of fear and half because he wasn't really such a bad egg, he agreed to take into his Kommando those inmates who were at the end of their ropes, those in grave danger of dying or being eliminated, which was the case with me. Milena, armed with a notice signed by Herr Schmidt, had the audacity to come and request that Syllinka turn over to her the inmate bearing registration number 27.372. To be sure, Syllinka had no idea which of the prisoners Milena was asking for, but she was still running a real risk not only for herself but for Schmidt as well. I spent several weeks among the piles of rabbit skins that were destined to serve as lining for the fur coats the SS troops would wear on the Eastern front against the Soviets. Then I was turned over by the heads of the camp resistance movement to one of the oldest German political prisoners in Ravensbrück, Maria Wittemeyer, who had the enormous responsibility of being in charge of the camp equipment and provisions. She was the one you had to go to if you wanted a few feet of cloth or a spool or two of cotton or wool thread. Thus she had the female guards—in fact, the entire camp hierarchy—in the palm of her hand, for they all had to go through her for anything they wanted on the camp black market. Maria received me without wasting any time on amenities.

"Up till now the only people I've taken on have been Communists," she said. "But the international committee has asked me to help save your life, so I'm making an exception. You can stay."

To be sure, Suhren had no notion of all these goings-on when he asked me where I worked, and I could see him wince when I told him I had been assigned to Syllinka's clothing workshop. For I had instinctively lifted my head and looked squarely at him. A redhead, he had a crafty air about him; he reminded me of a fox, which is not exactly flattering to that poor animal. He sat down on the edge of his desk and questioned me further.

"Which barracks are you in?"

"Block Thirty-one."

Another wince, even more obvious this time.

"Starting immediately, you're being assigned to the infirmary, and you'll be transferred to Block Two. I think you'll find it less arduous."

I took my courage in my hands and replied, "But I have no experience taking care of sick people."

"It doesn't matter. You'll be assigned to the record-keeping sector, since you know German."

The Kommandant picked up the telephone and called the head nurse, Frau Marschal, telling her that I would be joining the infirmary staff. Then he called the chief guard to inform her that I would be moving to a new barracks. I tried to protest that I preferred remaining with my French comrades in Block Thirty-one, but he would have none of it.

"That's an order," Suhren replied curtly.

Then, just as I was on the point of being escorted out of his office, he asked me again whether there was anything else I needed or wanted.

"Maybe some fresh underclothing? A warm jacket or sweater?"

"No, thank you, Kommandant, but as you well know the French women are among the most ill-treated in the camp. Their situation would be less impossible if they were all quartered in the same barracks. They're all in dire need of medicines and warm clothing to get through the winter."

"That's none of your business," he barked. "But if you personally are in need of anything else, let me know."

As I made my way back to my block, I rejoiced inwardly, not because of my changed situation, which was going to mean I'd be separated from my friends, but because I strongly suspected what their sudden interest in this poor, humble person, myself, had to mean: I was sure that the Kommandant's attention for prisoner number 27.372 was linked to the success of the Allied advance. Until then, no one among the SS personnel had the slightest inkling what my name was. If I had not yet succumbed to the beatings or the lack of food or hygiene, or died of exhaustion—not to mention perished in the "black convoy" that marched prisoners to their deaths—it was by pure chance.

That same evening I was transferred to Block Two, where there was only one other Frenchwoman, Baty, whose head had been entirely shorn of all its hair. Despite that, she had been assigned as the SS guards' hairdresser. In Block Two there was also a Belgian woman, a technician whose background and training had led her to be assigned to those workers whose job it was to repair the various camp equipment.

In any concentration camp, there was an amazing inequality among the inmates' situations. Completely stripped of all their goods and possessions when they arrived—having nothing, being nothing—occasionally one of them managed to acquire possessions or power, sometimes both. Each of the privileged prisoners in Block Two had her own straw mattress covered with a generously-filled eiderdown blanket with blue-and-white patchwork squares. Each of them also had her own little washcloth hung on her own hook in a closet, beside her metal mess tin and cup, and, to boot, even a spoon! They could—in fact were obliged to—keep themselves impeccably clean and completely free of lice, for their work put them in contact with the SS camp personnel. Moreover, Block Two was the showcase section of the Ravensbrück concentration camp, the place to which very special visitors or international inspection teams could be brought to show how life "really was" there.

The following day I received a clean camp dress, a jacket, a shawl, and a pair of pantines, a kind of wooden shoe that was almost new. Clearly, I was no longer a part of the camp's subproletariat, the lowest of the low, the ragged and tattered, those who were beaten at the drop of a hat, made to work overtime in one of the forced-labor battalions for some presumed infraction of the rules. And I was obliged to report to the head nurse of the infirmary, an ill-tempered woman who had been ordered to treat me equitably and had no choice but to comply with the Kommandant's orders. I shared a room with several other inmates—all of whom had been in the camp for a long time— a room that housed the camp archives. It was our job to update the deportees' records: the names and numbers of the living and dead. I didn't last very long at the job; after two days I fainted during roll call, and instead of being beaten till I struggled to my feet, which would normally have been my fate, I was taken just after the camp siren had ceased wailing to the main infirmary, not as a worker but as a patient. My scurvy sores were disinfected, I was given some vitamin pills, and I was exempted from roll call and allowed to remain in bed for several days. Then, on October 25, I was able to visit Jacqueline and a few friends in Block Thirty-one, in time to celebrate my twenty-fourth birthday. My new outfit was like a badge, the visible sign of my new status, which enabled me to move about the camp freely. Their clothing would never have permitted them to visit me in the "noble" part of the camp. Three days later when I was back in Block Two came the middle-of-the night SS visit, and I was trundled off to the bunker and my solitary confinement cell, where I was to remain for I knew not how long.

In any case, I took comfort in the fact

that the Kommandant himself had taken a personal interest in my case, which had to be a good sign. Now all I can do is wait. My fever is down, the pain in my side is less acute. Once again I glue my eye to the bullet-riddled crack in my cell door. Some soldiers are carting in some furniture; in the cell across the corridor from mine but one floor above, they bring in a man who is in uniform but without SS insignia. He is not wearing a cap, but I have a feeling he's an officer of some kind. In the past I've been allowed one walk a day, but now they have upped it to two, and since my new neighbor's cell door has been left open, I note that the food they are serving him is not the normal camp rations.

When I get back from my walk, his cell door is closed. As I enter my cell, the woman guard hands me a letter. Joy, tears of joy: I can see that it's in my father's handwriting. Therefore he's alive and knows where I am. I read and reread the address on the envelope:

> To Prisoner De Gaulle Geneviève
> No. 27.372   Block 26
> F. K. L. Ravensbrück (near
> Fürstenberg)
> Mecklenburg, Germany

Then I turn the envelope over and read the return address:

> Xavier de Gaulle
> 27 rue Plantamour
> Geneva, Switzerland

When my fingers stop shaking so badly, I carefully open the letter, which is the first one I've received since my arrest. My father has written in German. What foresight to have learned the language of Goethe! His sentences are short and simple, and he has given me the rundown on each member of the family, including my brother Roger, who is fighting with the Free French Forces. To celebrate the event, I give my cockroaches some extra rations, an oversized chunk of bread, but I also make an extra effort to down a bit of soup, to try to build up my strength at least a bit. My arms and my legs are still emaciated, even more than before; my open sores still refuse to heal. But that doesn't keep me from having a wonderful dream. I'm lying on my stomach on a flat-bottomed boat on very dark water. The stream is narrow, bounded on both sides by steep black rocks that descend sharply to the river's edge. The current bears me along through an endless tunnel that is so low I can't even lift my head. And then suddenly, at the very end, there is a light, ever so faint, and I wake up, my heart filled with renewed hope. A long day, just like so many others, but somehow differ-ent. I sing the *Lieder* that Father taught me, he at the piano as my accompanist: "The Trout," "The Lore," "The Old Lin-den Tree," "The King of Aulnes." I also say a prayer, harking back to the one he included in his letter when he talked to me about my dear sweet mother and my sister Jacqueline.

A woman guard has just come into my cell. She looks at me with neither hostility nor disdain. Have I perhaps become in her eyes a human being? Without a word of explanation, she sets on my little table some Calcium D Redoxon tablets and three boxes of C Phosphate. The medicines are from Switzerland, and the boxes they come in strike me as positively luxurious. It's as though a dream has come true. I begin taking the calcium pills immediately, but decide to hold off a bit for the vitamins. Anna has brought me some mending work to do and a pair of scissors. I take the scissors and, from the ice-cold cardboard box in which the medicines were packed, cut out a tiny set of playing cards for myself, marking them with my pencil stub so that I can have a game of solitaire now and then.

Today marks the first anniversary of our departure from Fresnes Prison. At the clerk's office one year ago, they returned to us some of the objects that were confiscated upon our arrival. They gave me my red-and-black purse, which contained a bit of tobacco and my pipe; my glasses; and some photographs that turned out not to be mine. What they failed to return were my gold watch, which my godmother had given me; my pretty ring, with a topaz set in a crown of little pearls, which had been a gift from my aunt Madeleine on my twenty-first birthday; and the small amount of cash I had on me the day I was arrested. On the eve of our departure, in the ground-floor cells to which we had all been transferred, we had been delighted—despite the uncertainty of our fate—to discover at long last the faces of our fellow prisoners, whom to that point we had known only by the sound of their voices.

Transferred from Fresnes to the Royaillieu Camp near Compiègne, we found upon our arrival hundreds and hundreds of other women prisoners from every corner of France. The barracks, which had been hastily constructed, were, to say the least, rudimentary. We each had a bowl and were given half a liter of water a day to drink and wash with as we saw fit. The latrines were a long way away, a ditch dug into the ground right next to the metal fence that separated the women's section from that of the men. But within the confines of our own area we were free to move about at will, to speak with whomever we wanted. I was amazed to discover the range and diversity of my fellow prisoners: young and old, from very different backgrounds and geographic locations. Virtually all of them had been arrested for their involvement in the Resistance, but their reasons for joining the Underground were many and varied: their common bond was their unanimous refusal to accept the defeat of their country at the hands of the Nazis. Some belonged to the intelligence units, others had housed and hidden Allied aviators who were shot down over France, still others had given refuge to those clandestinely sent by the Free French Forces from London into France to reconnoiter and report back. Pauline, whom I had liked the moment I met her, was a worker and a Communist who had actively participated in sabotages and attempted assassinations. Bella, who was the daughter of a family of diplomats, had just been released from several months of solitary confinement. Shaking her beautiful head of black hair, she recited to us the poems she had written in her cell in the depths of Fresnes. Claire, a professor and, politically, a Socialist, had been involved with the Underground hero Pierre Brossolette and had met the legendary Jean Moulin. Odette told us about the tortures to which her sixteen-year-old son had been subjected. Between two painful moans, he had cried out, "Don't talk, Mother, don't tell them anything!" Yvonne was a doctor; Annie was the wife of the permanent secretary of the French Institute. Lola, who was a monarchist, owned the bookstore on the rue Bonaparte in Paris called Au voeu de Louis XIII, which also served as the drop for the Resistance movement known as "Defense of France," where I, among several others, had been arrested on July 20, 1943.

How can I cite only these few, when all their faces press in upon me? They invaded my cell, they called out, they applauded when my name was called out to leave for the waiting train. The Germans were furious at the women's reaction, which they did not understand (we were not yet dealing with the SS), but they reacted by pushing and shoving us and by siccing several dogs on us, trying to scare us to death. But we felt, before we were pushed and locked into the waiting cattle cars, both very strong and, yes, oh so fragile!

The trip lasted three days and three nights. Not a drop of water to drink; as toilet, an oil drum that was supposed to serve the eighty women in the car, who could neither stretch out nor even sit down except a few at a time. None of them will ever be able to forget the night the cattle-car train came to a halt in the dark of night: it was the night of February 2 and 3. At long last the train door slid open; we were all in a state of total exhaustion, barely cognizant, but we were brought quickly back to our senses by the angry shouts of the SS and the barking of their dogs. We had to jump down out of the cars; fortunately the ground beneath was sandy, but that was more than offset by the truncheon blows that greeted us.

"Hurry up, hurry it up, by rows of five, you dirty bitches!" they shouted.

"What are they saying?" some of my neighbors, who spoke no German, wanted to know.

I translated the gist of their words, stressing the need to line up in rows of five.

For better or worse, the long column

set off through pine woods whose trees were dusted with a light layer of snow. After what seemed like an interminable lapse of time, we finally marched through the main gate of the camp. Where were we? How was this unreal trek through the night going to end?

Now we know the answer to that question, but who from our convoy will remain alive to tell the tale? How many of my comrades have died since I was sent down here to the bunker? And what has happened to those who were shipped off to the various work Kommandos?

Right now, sometime before the morning siren for roll call sounds, I hear some movement to and fro in the corridor. Once again I glue my eye to the crack in my cell door and see my neighbor, the man in the cell upstairs directly opposite mine, being led from his cell flanked by two SS guards. For a fleeting moment I see his stoic face, his short-clipped salt-and-pepper hair, and I am overcome by a feeling that he is heading toward death, that he will never come back to the bunker again. However that may be, I bid him adieu.

In the course of the day, one of the woman guards comes to tell me that I should gather up my belongings.

"They're transferring you to another cell," she says.

I cast a last look around my somber lodging, at my cockroaches, with not a tinge of nostalgia or regret. The woman guard returns and, noticing Felix crouching next to me, raises her shoe and crushes him with a look of utter disgust on her face. We go up a staircase at the far end of a corridor. The new cell to which I've been assigned is directly across from my old one, one flight up: the cell of my unknown neighbor whose departure I had witnessed just a few hours before.

The bright light of the declining sun suddenly blinds me, burning my eyes. The window of the cell looks directly onto the wall that separates the camp from the crematorium ovens. The horrible odor fills my lungs and, depending on which way the wind is blowing, invades my entire domain. The meager furnishings of my new cell are exactly as same as those downstairs. Whatever extras they may have installed for the previous guest must have been removed. I notice, just beyond the little cell window, a piece of wrapping paper sticking out. Feeling a trifle stronger than before, I manage to drag my little wooden stool, which luckily is not chained to the wall, over to the window. Climbing up on it, I can see in the distance, far beyond the camp wall, the tops of some pine trees. And indeed, between the window pane and the outside cell bars, there is a straw case, the kind they use to protect wine bottles, and inside is a piece of paper all wrinkled up. With great difficulty I manage to fish the paper from its straw container and climb down off my stool to read the name of the person for whom it was intended: General von . . . Will I ever learn the reasons that led to this man's being incarcerated in a women's concentration camp and whatever became of him?

Without question, I am feeling better, thanks to the calcium and the light—even if my eyes are starting to hurt again—and for the third time today I am taken out into the courtyard for a walk. But this time the sky is blue, with a slightly pearly luster to it; the air is bracing, and I have the feeling that I am emerging from a deep, dark cave. Now I don't feel indifferent about whether I live or die. I want to see my loved ones again, another spring, the trees all in bloom. When I get back to Paris, I'm going to the Orangerie to gaze again at Monet's *Water Lilies.* Just by forcing myself to think about it, the flowers have filled my dreams; their luminously bright corollas have completely covered my silent lake.

The odor of the crematoriums is becoming intolerable. Pungent smoke fills my cell. I point it out to Anna, and she responds succinctly by informing me that one of the two ovens, which were impossibly jam-packed with bodies, caught on fire. So you see, I had fantasized my escape from the camp a trifle too soon. The truth is, the number of corpses is increasing with every passing day. Even before I was taken down to the bunker, they had constructed a second crematorium oven right next to the first; we had watched as the chimney rose higher and higher above the wall of the camp. And even a second oven, it would appear, did not suffice.

"They're all going to die," Anna said with a deep sigh as she handed me my coffee through the grill of the cell door.

Why am I not with the others? This willful separation is becoming more and more unbearable for me, and my thoughts forever take me back inside the camp. For several nights running I have had the same obsessive dream: They come to fetch me from my cell and put me into a car that keeps driving on and on through the shadows of night. Then, suddenly, I am in a blinding light: I am being arraigned before some kind of tribunal. The judges, all dressed in dark robes, are wearing magistrates' caps, their faces completely expressionless. I am told that I am to describe life in the Ravensbrück concentration camp. It is very important; that I know. But as I start to tell them what it's like, I see that my deposition is rife with all sorts of gaps and memory blanks. Each time I wake up from that dream, my throat is constricted and I have the terrible feeling that I'm simply not up to the task. Powerless. Now my days are spent carefully completing my indictment. I only want to testify to what I saw with my own eyes, what I personally experienced . . . and that is atrocious. Little by little, my memory reconstitutes what until now I have done my best to forget simply in order to survive. My accusation becomes more and more precise, laid out in my mind in a logical sequence. In my dream, I go on facing my impassive judges.

Suddenly, my cell door opens and Suhren himself materializes before me. I have seen him only one other time since my meeting at the Kommandantur on October 3, the night of my arrival at the bunker. No, I am not dreaming; he is speaking to me, and I have the feeling he is less arrogant, a trifle less haughty than before.

"You are about to receive a visit," he tells me. "Two gentlemen. They will ask you a number of questions, all of which you should answer accurately and candidly."

Scarcely has he finished speaking when two men appear. Suhren has chairs brought in for them. One of the men is a civilian, rather coarse looking, very self-assured. He is wearing a black felt hat, has a fat blue emerald ring on his finger, an emerald *en cabochon,* and I note that his elegant shoes are impeccably polished. The other is a fairly young soldier with no SS insignia; he immediately removes his cap and looks at me attentively. I somehow get the impression he's a doctor. After having made a sign for me to sit down on my bed, Suhren perches on my stool and repeats to me that I'm to answer all the questions that are asked of me with complete candor, after which he does not open his mouth again, obviously very impressed by the two others.

The interview begins with questions about how I was arrested, the circumstances surrounding my arrest, whether I had any complaints to make with regard to my interrogation at the hands of the Gestapo, how I was treated during my incarceration at Fresnes Prison. I specify that while I had not been personally tortured, I had been knocked to the ground, where I had been kicked and beaten, which seems to shock the note-taking officer. Then I bring up the terrible voyage in the cattle cars, the arrival at Ravensbrück, the anguish at being stripped naked, the dogs, the beatings, the terror. After which, trying to follow a strict chronological order, I describe the progressive destruction of what constitutes a human being: depriving her of her dignity, her relations with her fellow creatures, her most basic rights. We are *Stücke*—pieces. Even our fellow inmates—some of whom have positions as guards, policewomen, barrack chiefs—can with impunity insult and revile us, beat us, trample us under foot, kill us. As far as anyone in the camp hierarchy is concerned, it's good riddance: one vermin less to deal with. I have seen, I have experienced, this willful oppression, this grinding down of a fellow human being who is in such a state of exhaustion she can barely move. At the end of her rope. Hunger, cold, forced labor—

all are ordeals we have to endure, but they are far from the worst.

What do my visitors make of all this? Are they able to grasp what I'm saying? Every once in a while one of them starts from his seat and asks me to clarify one point or another, especially when the abuses I'm describing affect me personally. Perhaps Suhren realizes that this inmate is still capable of testifying and even of passing judgment. If Nazi Germany is defeated, many among those in charge will doubtless be held accountable. Unless all those who might testify against these leaders are eliminated, down to the very last one. Is this deposition meant to test me, to ascertain how forceful and convincing my accusation might be later if I ever get out of Ravensbrück alive?

I have no idea how long this strange interrogation lasts. Later we leave my cell and repair to the SS infirmary, hard by the Kommandantur. Now the young doctor is leading the inquest, in the presence of the camp's Dr. Trommer, whom I had seen once before when I had an attack of pleurisy. The young doctor asks for my medical record. . . . What a joke! He waxes indignant when he notes that after I was given an X-ray that found my lungs in terrible shape, nothing whatsoever was done about it. He is also shocked at the visible signs of scurvy I'm displaying—anemia, bleeding from the mucous membranes—as he is by how emaciated I am and how weak. Clearly I am not a model reference for the Ravensbrück Camp! The medical examination is interrupted by an air-raid alert, and I am hustled back to my cell; this whole thing strikes me as completely surreal. Not any more surreal, however, than my interrogation by one of the high-ranking members of the Gestapo whose offices are located beyond the confines of the camp proper. I am received there by a man who is pointedly courteous and who without further ado begins talking to me about Paris, where he has spent several months.

"I have such fond memories of your city," he tells me.

He quickly learns, however, that I don't exactly share his enthusiasm for the members of the Gestapo with whom I came into contact in Paris, and he moves quickly on to a rundown of my activities in the French Resistance movement. I do my best to minimize my role, and though he keeps pressing, I steadfastly refuse to reveal any of my comrades' names. We're a long way from Paris, but you never know! There still may be members of the Underground who have not yet been captured, whose files are still open. A secretary who is wearing very thick makeup and who tends to smile a great deal is typing up this strange interrogatory, which I quickly understand is more a formality than anything else. When she is finished, the gentleman from the Gestapo hands me my deposition, asks me to read it over and verify that it is correct, and then departs, leaving me and the secretary alone for a few minutes.

As soon as he leaves, the secretary begins speaking to me in French—it turns out that she, too, adores Paris.

"Would you mind very much inscribing something in French in my album?" she asks. "Just a few lines, in remembrance of our meeting."

Since I'm clearly perplexed by her request, the young woman suggests:

"For instance, the beginning of a song by Lucienne Boyer, whom I adore!"

And so I write, as though it were someone else performing the task:

"'*Parlez-moi d'amour, dites-moi les choses tendres. . . .*' 'Speak to me of love, whisper me sweet nothings' Lucienne Boyer."

And under Lucienne Boyer's name I add my own:

"Geneviève de Gaulle."

When the Gestapo officer comes back

into the room, the secretary falls silent again, then hands me the report of my "confession" for another signature. By the time I'm returned to my normal abode, night is falling.

I don't dream anymore, however; I find it almost impossible to sleep. Smoke is still pouring from the crematorium smokestacks; the ritual sounds of the camp are muted by the time they reach my ears. Outside my window, fat, lazy snowflakes are falling. To try to keep myself busy, I decide to arrange the few personal objects I've been able to retain: my Christmas souvenirs; my little pouch where my needles are stored, a present from Jacqueline; my little deck of playing cards; a few thin sheets of writing paper; the pouch where I keep my meager ration of bread; the three green, triangular boxes in which I keep my vitamin C pills. And it's a good thing I put everything in order. The very next day the female guard will burst into my cell and switch on the light, yelling, "On your feet! Get yourself dressed! And be quick about it!"

She has brought me a navy-blue dress with white painted stripes, some linen sandals, and—miracle of miracles!—my very own coat. Yes, the same coat my friends had somehow managed to have delivered to me when I was still in Fresnes Prison, in anticipation of my upcoming voyage to Germany—the coat I had been obliged to turn in to the authorities when we arrived at the camp. I slip on the coarse wool stockings that Lisa knitted, which fit snugly into the summer sandals, and wrap myself in the soft brown shawl— the gift from my fellow prisoners—before slipping on my coat. I cannot tell you the pleasure I felt when I put on that coat! I take the little piece of cloth I have been using as a napkin, place on it the few pos- sessions I am taking with me, fold it, and knot it shut. My mess kit and cup will have to remain behind, as will my prison dress. A few moments later I leave my cell—perhaps forever? I have the feeling that I've spent entire years there, lived several lives within its walls. Anna is standing silently in the corridor. In her hand she is holding the little handkerchief I gave her at Christmas, which she waves discreetly as a way of bidding me good-bye.

In the bunker office, two SS officers await me, as well as a younger female guard and another, terribly emaciated woman who looks absolutely ancient. On her shaven skull, a rare tuft of hair has regrown here and there. She looks like Gandhi at the end of his life. We exchange glances for a brief moment but don't dare exchange words; I take her hand as we descend the three steps of the bunker. Together, surrounded by the SS officers and the young female guard, we pass through the camp gate. It is still snowing, and the wind is like ice. I try to look back, and from afar I can see the silhouettes of several women, all stooped over, carrying heavy vats of coffee. Dawn is just breaking. Could it perchance be the dawn of hope?